CLASSICAL INDIAN SCULPTURE

CLASSICAL
INDIAN SCULPTURE

300 B.C. *to* A.D. *500*

by

CHINTAMONI KAR

1950

ALEC TIRANTI LTD.
72 CHARLOTTE STREET,
LONDON, W.1

Made and printed in Great Britain

PREFACE

The purpose of this little book is to introduce classical Indian sculpture, and the examples shown have been selected chiefly because of their sculptural qualities. The book is too small to include detailed information, but the short bibliography will perhaps be useful to the reader for further study.

In spite of recent excavations, the dating of the various schools cannot be regarded as final. The dates, particularly of Gandhara, Kushan, Mathura, and Amaravati are controversial. Further excavation and discoveries may change the dates usually accepted for the Kushan and Andhra periods. It is not always possible to fix the date of a sculpture from its general appearance, as throughout Indian history it has been the custom to restore old and damaged work as nearly as possible in the same style of the original. But at the same time the sculptors would introduce contemporary motives of their own age. Thus, some work presents an extraordinary mixture of style, and is difficult to date. This copying of the old style is still practised all over India, where old shrines are in use.

The writer owes thanks to the authorities of the Royal Academy of Arts, India Office Library, British Museum, Indian Section of the Victoria and Albert

Museum, Royal Scottish Museum, Birmingham
Museum and Art Gallery; to Major-General H. L.
Haughton, C.B., C.I.E., C.B.E., Col. D. H. Gordon,
D.S.O., O.B.E., Capt. John Hay of Hayfield, Messrs.
Spink & Sons, Ltd., for their generous permission to
reproduce photographs of pieces in their collections,
and special thanks to Mr. and Mrs. Wint for reading
the manuscript.

LONDON, 1950.   C. K.

vi

CONTENTS

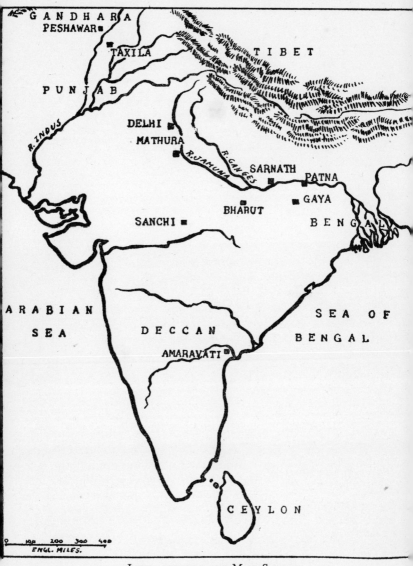

INDIA, SHOWING THE MAIN SITES.

I.

Historical outline.

IN ancient India sculpture developed and flourished long before the time of which we have archæological record. The abundant collection of statuettes in stone, bronze and terra-cotta, found in the buried cities of Mohenjo Daro in Sindh and Harappa in the Punjab, dates back almost certainly to the third millenium B.C., but this Indo-Sumerian art does not seem to have any links with that of the later period of the so-called Vedic time. The earliest specifically Indian sculptures in existence belong to 3rd century B.C., though there are references to various artistic crafts in literature before this time.

What is known as " classical " Indian sculpture is that which was produced from the time of the MAURYAN dynasty, which flourished in the 4th century B.C. until the time of the GUPTA dynasty in the 5th century A.D.

It will help to make the development clearer if the historical framework is grouped at the outset.

Alexander the Great invaded India in the year 326 B.C. Partly as a reaction to this invasion, a great Empire grew up shortly afterwards in North India. This was the famous Mauryan Empire. Its greatest king was Asoka, who reigned from 273 B.C. to 232 B.C. His capital was at Pataliputra, the modern Patna.

It is from this period that dates the first major sculpture which still survives. Asoka was either a

Buddhist or very friendly to Buddhism. To extol the glory of the faith, he erected numerous monuments in the places which had been sanctified by the birth, preaching, or passing away of the mortal Buddha, or where the Buddhist relics were buried. Nothing has remained of Asoka's imperial palace at his capital, but old Greek and Roman travellers describe its splendours as unparalleled and excelling the beauties of the royal palaces of Susa and Ekbatana. The palace was built on a foundation of unbaked bricks, protected perhaps with a stone facing, and the superstructure was of wood. It was certainly decorated with sculpture and painting. The narratives in the old literature are full of vivid descriptions of such royal dwellings and they cannot be ignored as fanciful. In the bas reliefs of the old Buddhist monuments there are illustrations of cities and palaces which fully bear out the ancient accounts (Figs. 25, 26).

After Asoka's death in 232 B.C., the power of the dynasty declined. In the last half of the 2nd century B.C., power passed to the new dynasty called the SUNGAS. The Sunga kings were probably not Buddhists, but they patronised Buddhist art. A number of important shrines survive from that period.

From the 3rd century B.C. until the 2nd century A.D. there was a very unsettled time in North India. The Sunga Empire fell to pieces, and in the North-West there rose Greek kingdoms which had been established by the successors of Alexander the Great. These were succeeded by Greek and Parthian rulers. Many of these foreign princes in India became followers of Brahminism and Buddhism, as well perhaps, as retaining their original faith.* Thus, there took place a great intermingling of religion and culture, which had a deep influence on Indian art. Zoroastrian, Greek, Mithraic and other foreign iconographies were all assimilated by India.

In the 1st century A.D. a great empire rose in North India under the KUSHANS, who were a branch of the Yueh chi nomads. Their great king was Kanishka, who ruled from 120 A.D. to 162 A.D.

During this time rose the two celebrated schools of sculpture, Gandhara and Mathura. The Gandhara, the school of the frontier, takes its name from the ancient word for the geographical area comprising the valley of the Kabul river and the north-western provinces of India. The speciality of this school was its Græco-Indian sculpture of Buddha. The old Greek colonies planted in the north-west from the time of Alexander onwards thus left their trace on that area.

* " Of the monumental records of the Bactrian Greeks in India, only one has yet been found, and that is not in Greek, but in the early Brahmi script of India. This inscription, which was found in the ancient city of Vidisa in Central India—1,000 miles away from Taxila—is carved on the face of a pillar, and tells us that the pillar was set up by a Greek named Heliodorus, the son of Dion, who came as ambassador to Vidisa from Antialcidas, the Greek king of Taxila. Incidentally, this inscription shows us how the Greeks were then embracing the religions of the country of their adoption. With their very elastic pantheon they readily identified Indian gods with their own deities; and, just as in Italy they identified Minerva with Athena or Baccus with Dionysus, so in India they identified the Sun-god Surya with Apollo and Kama, the god of Love, with their own Eros ; and they had no hesitation, therefore, in paying their devotions to Siva or to Parvati, to Vishnu or to Lakshmi."

A Guide to Taxila, by Sir John Marshall.

The Mathura school was based on the city which still survives. Here, too, the speciality was the Buddhist statuary and also Jaina images. But the Greek influence did not reach here. The style was more purely Indian.

While these dynasties and these schools of art were flourishing in north India, there had been a different development in the south. A dynasty called the ANDHRAS had been established in the Deccan since the time of Asoka. The dynasty remained in power for five centuries, and was a great benefactor to Buddhism. From this dynasty survive the splendid gateways of Sanchi and the famous remains at Amaravati.

At the beginning of the 3rd century A.D. the reigns of the Andhras in the Deccan and the Kushans in northern India came to an end. All vassal states under their paramountcy declared their independence. Many claimants to the vacant imperial power waged war against their neighbouring states, and thus a political and social chaos swept the whole country. There is no record of any great art or literary productions during this unrest. After a century's disturbances, Chandragupta, the king of Magadha, brought the whole of northern India, except the Punjab, under his sway and established a strong imperial dynasty and peace. His successors enlarged his dominion and became great patrons of art, literature, music, drama and science. Indian culture never achieved a greater refinement or brilliance than during this period. All loose and divergent ideas and motifs of art were brought to a

4

synthetic and harmonised order, and the visible foreign elements were either completely diffused or lost in the Indianised patterns, or were categorically omitted by the Gupta sculptors.

II.

Early Icons and Maurya art.

Though it is predominently Buddhist, Mauryan art is influenced by old Brahminical and West-Asian motifs. Images connected with nature worship were very common in this early period. The cult of mother-goddess existed even before the time of the Vedas; it is the giver of fertility and fortune, and is represented by the Brahminical image Lakshmi or Sri and the Buddhist Sirima Devata. Other motifs have an origin no less ancient. There are the Yakshas and Yakshinis; these are super-human powers and spirits of the earth resembling mortal men and women. There are Nagas or the snake people, the spirits of water living in the lakes and rivers. There are the Apsaras, divine nymphs who, according to the Rig Veda, are " the personifications of the vapours which are attracted by the sun and form into mist and clouds," and, according to another account, were born of the ocean when it was churned by the gods to obtain Amrita (nectar). There are the Lokapalas, the guardians of the quarters.

The chief sculptures surviving from the Maurya period are the capitals of Asoka's pillars. These pillars are huge monolithic stone shafts with a very highly polished surface. The capitals contain a

Persepolitan bell-shaped lotus, surmounted with four addrosed lions which supported a wheel (now lost), the symbol of the first preaching of Buddha, ecclesiastically called " The Wheel of the Law "* a bull which represents the nativity of Buddha since he was born under the Zodiacal constellations Taurus; an elephant, the symbol of conception, and a horse (there is no specimen of this in existence now), representing his renunciation (i.e., his great departure from home). The edge of the bell-formed lotus is usually decorated with bas-reliefs of wild geese or floral motifs, or the four animals mentioned above. The superb modelling of the figures shows skilful blending of realistic form with idealised signs of power and dignity. In the whole history of Indian sculpture the Mauryan carvers were never surpassed in the precision and mastery of chiselling stone.

Besides the Asokan pillars, there have survived a few colossal sandstone figures almost in the round. These represent Yakshas and Yakshinis. Most of

* " In the primitive period, the spoked-wheel is referred to as the grandest kind of work of the Vedic Aryans. And for the primitive man, the construction of a spoked wheel does, indeed, betoken a vast stride forwards. In the Rigveda the Wheel (with its spokes, of which ' none is the last ') and its form are favourite similes, and often representations. ' The much-lauded Indra ' (thus it says in the Rigveda, vii, 32, 20) ' I incline by means of the song, as a cartwright bends the rim of a wheel made of good wood ; ' or (Sakra) ' the lightning in his hand, rules over all men, as the rim of a wheel embraces the spokes ' (Rigv. i, 32, 35). It would carry us too far to follow out all the similes ; the wheel remains in the Indian civilised world of antiquity, and even down to modern times, as symbol of occult power, the theme for grand poetical similes. The Buddhists took the wheel, as we shall see below, as one of the distinctive emblems of their religion."

Buddhist art in India, by A. Grünwedel, translated by A. C. Gibson.

these monolithic statues have an archaic appearance, but express great virility and life. Their skilful carving and technical maturity suggests that there must have been a long prior development and practise of sculpture in India.

The statue of a female fly-whisk bearer is a fine example of these monumental figures. The figure is nude to the waist except that she wears elaborate jewellery. Her head is finely portrayed, and she has a well-modelled torso. The very full and heavy breasts and comparatively slender waist probably show the conventional idea of feminine beauty of the time. In spite of the general robustness of the figure, the treatment of the ornaments and drapery is very delicate (Figs. 7, 8).

III.

Sunga art.

The chief monuments of this period are the stone railings and sculpture of the Buddhist shrines at Bharut, Bodhgaya and Sanchi. These are commonly known as stupas. They were erected on sites which had been sanctified by the presence of Buddha during his life, or where his and other Buddhist saints' remains were buried.

Apart from the stupa ballustrades, there are few specimens of Sunga sculpture. For some unknown reasons the Mauryan technique of polishing the stone so that it acquired a glossy surface is not found in Sunga or later art. Some fragmentary Sunga human heads and statuettes show that the Sunga style varied from the Maurya. But even the smallest of these figures in stone and terra-cotta maintains the monumental quality of the earlier school. The Sunga stone heads found in the vicinity of Sarnath monastery were probably the portraits of the donors. Each of them has a distinctive head-dress giving an admirable expression of individuality (Fig. 6).

The Buddhists were not the only sect which built stupas over the relics of their saints. There were also the Jains. The Jain religion is as old as the Buddhist and has almost similar doctrines. The founders of both the Buddhist and Jain religions were princes who renounced thrones to enter into monastic life. Many Jain divinities are identical with the Buddhists' gods and goddesses. In addition to Buddhism and Jainism, the Brahminical faith also had a very large following all over India at the time. But the Buddhists probably received their most powerful support from the kings, and this enabled them to build monasteries and stupas on a grand scale, using stone and other expensive materials and enlisting the services of skilled artisans. They also received large gifts from rich merchants and the guilds of craftsmen.

IV.

Bharut Stupa.

Bharut stupa is believed to have existed in Asoka's time and definitely was built during the Sunga rule. Situated between Allahabad and Jabbalpur, the site of Bharut may have been that of an important city. But the ancient geography of this part of India is too obscure for there to be any certainty. Except for the solitary pillars, coping stones and a section of the railing, there is nothing left of the original mound. From the bas-relief illustrations on the railing it can be seen that the old stupa was a hemispherical solid dome standing on a cylindrical base. On the top of this dome there was a flat platform enclosed with a stone railing and a stone umbrella (Tee) fixed at the centre. There was a processional path round the stupa fenced by a circle of ballustrade of massive stones. This stone railing had openings at the cardinal points and was decorated with pillared gateways. Sir A. Cunningham gave a very interesting account of the stupa as follows: —

" The subjects represented in the Bharut sculptures are both numerous and varied, and many of them are of the highest interest and importance for the study of Indian history. Thus we have more than a score of illustrations of the legendary Jatakas, and some half-dozen illustrations of historical scenes connected with the life of Buddha, which are quite invaluable for the history of Buddhism. Their value is chiefly due to the inscribed labels that are attached to many of them, and which make their identification absolutely certain. Amongst the historical scenes, the most interesting are the processions of the Rajas Ajatasatru, and Prosenjita on their visits to Buddha; the former on his elephant, the latter in his chariot, exactly as they are described in the Buddhist chronicles. Another invaluable sculpture is the representation of the famous Jetavana monastery at Sravasti—with its mango tree, temples and the rich banker Anathpindika in the foreground emptying a cartful of gold pieces to pave the surface of the garden (Fig. 15).

" Of large figures there are upwards of thirty alto-relievo statues of Yakshas and Yakshinis, Devatas, Naga Rajas, one half of which are inscribed with their names. We thus see that the guardianship of the North Gate was entrusted to Kuvera, King of the Yakshas, agreeably to the teaching of the Buddhist and Brahminical cosmogonies. And similarly we find that the other gates were confided to the Devas and Nagas.

" The representations of animals and trees are also very numerous, and some of them are particularly spirited and characteristic. Of other subjects there are boats, horse-chariots and bullock-carts, besides several kinds of musical instruments, and a great variety of flags, standards and other symbols of royalty."

According to some scholars, the bell-shaped lotus capitals supporting lions and the bulls, and inscriptions in *Kharoshthi* type, suggest that Western artists must have been employed by the donors to design and execute those gates. But it is quite certain that the railing of Bharut was worked by the local artists. The corner pillars of the entrances have almost life-size figures in very high relief. These represent Yakshas, Yakshinis, Nagas and other demigod characters, who act as the guardians of the monument. These statues exhibit the sculptor's fine sense of balance. Their bold modelling and mono-

10

lithic monumental quality are imbued with warmth and charm of life (Figs. 12, 13, 14).

The sculptures of the coping and the rails are in very flat relief but the contours of each object are prominently carved. There is no hazy superimposition in the illustrations. For centuries past, sculpture must have been in wood, and this produced a marked effect on these reliefs. It is curious that the change from working in wood to working in stone did not alter the general style in sculpture until two or three hundred years after Bharut had been carved. These sculptures tell a story, describing scenes from Jatakas (the stories of Buddha's previous lives), and historical events relating to Buddhism. These are portrayals in a simple folk art. The landscapes show trees and forests, lakes and rivers and various aquatic animals, elephants, deer, monkeys and birds. There are human figures in a palace, a procession, domestic and monastic scenes. But there is no suggestion of perspective or horizon. All the objects are shown successively in semi-bird's-eye view. There is no battle theme or picture of conflict such as appear in later stupas. The friezes of these sculptures reveal only festival events and peaceful serenity (Figs. 10, 11, 15, 16). The theism of the Buddhists, which was later to show Buddha in person as a god, is totally absent in the Bharut imagery. His mortal presence in the theme is represented by symbols—by his footprint, by the throne on which he sat, by the sacred tree under which he received enlightenment, and by the stupa, referring to Buddha's *Parinirvana*. Buddha is not shown in person.

V.

Sanchi.

The most magnificent of all Buddhist monuments still *in situ* are the stupas at Sanchi. These are almost hemispherical domes with truncated tops and are surrounded by a high terraced base. As at Bharut, the stupas are encircled at ground level by a processional path, which is fenced with a ballustrade of massive stones. The greatest of these mounds has four fine lofty gateways adjoining the ballustrade and almost at the cardinal points. These monuments date as far back as the time of king Asoka. That they were of considerable importance is proved by the protection and patronage given to them by five or more imperial dynasties, covering nearly thirteen centuries.

The best sculptures and the superb gates of the great stupa were erected during the Andhra dynasty which ruled the Deccan from 2nd or 1st century B.C. to 3rd century A.D. Probably in the early period the ballustrade and gates had been made up of wood. When they perished, they were replaced by stone erections modelled after the old structure. This may be the explanation of their strange appearance, for though made of stone, they resemble wood or ivory. In fact, one of the gates bears an inscription that it was executed by the ivory carvers of Vidisha (Fig. 17).

The gates are, in general structure, alike, but the subjects and details of the sculptures differ considerably. Each gate has a richly carved superstructure of three slightly arched stone beams with volute ends, fixed horizontally on two high square pillars. These pillars also bear numerous reliefs on all faces. The capitals of the pillars supporting the architraves contain massive figures of dwarf Yakshas, elephants and lotuses. It is amazing that these delicately ornamented, top-heavy constructions have remained intact on two comparatively slender columns for about two thousand years. The architraves between their three tiers hold caryatids of Yakshinis and figures of horsemen, and elephants with riders. These images are carved on all sides and may be the earliest examples of Indian sculpture in the round. The Yakshini, gracefully reclining against the mango tree, appears to be nude apart from the heavy collar, bangles, anklets and the be-jewelled girdle she wears; there is a suggestion of flimsy cloth between her waist and her knee, clinging to the form (Fig. 33). The faces of the pillars are elaborately carved with floral decoration and with illustrations of the Jatakas in relief (Figs. 18, 19, 20, 21). The lotus, symbol of the birth of Buddha, appears on all the railings. The figure of Sri, or Lakshmi—the pre-Buddhist mother-goddess, which was later adopted to assume the rôle of Mayadevi (mother of mortal Buddha)—is represented on the architraves. She is seated or standing on a lotus, and elephants are spraying holy water over her (Fig. 34). Many compositions showing human, animal forms and plant motifs have a strong West-Asian affinity (Figs. 32, 35). The central panels of the architraves have scenes crowded with human and animal

13

figures in the palace or forest. These depict Jatakas. Another motif is the "war of the relics." This occurred when the Malla clans of Kusinara came into possession of the remains of Buddha when he passed away in their territory. Seven chiefs of other clans waged war against the Mallas, claiming a share of the relics. The conflict was ended by giving equal shares of the sacred remains to each militant chief. It is said that king Asoka recovered most of the remains of Buddha and divided them into 84,000 parts, over which he erected stupas in various sites within his dominion.

Many writers on Indian sculpture have inferred that the Persepolitan animal and floral motifs found on the Sanchi gates were carried out by foreign artists. But this ought not to be accepted simply because of their apparent outlandish look. Long before the conquest of Alexander the Great, trade routes were in existence between India and the countries of West Asia to the west of the city of Susa. With the exchange of art commodities among the trading countries, new styles and ideas were naturally imported and were gradually absorbed into the native art and tradition. The lion capitals of Asoka pillars may have been introduced by Græco-Persian art. But in the hands of the Indian carvers they became completely Indian in spirit and execution.*

* "It is important in the history of ancient Buddhist sculptures to remember the political relations which prevailed between the Kingdom of Achæmenides and N.W. India. Darius (old Persian Daryavaush), son of Hystaspes, was the first king of the dynasty regarding whose territorial acquisitions and explorations in India we have trustworthy information. After this king, in great

VI.

Gandhara School.

The next principal art periods after the end of the Sunga school were those of Gandhara and Mathura. The achievement of the Gandhara school was to introduce novel ideas and style, and the new Buddhist divinities which hitherto had had only symbolical existence. New images emerged of Buddha clad in ascetic robe and in yogic attitudes, and Bodhisattvas in princely attire. Sakya Muni was shown as a child, prince, ascetic and preacher. He became the principal character in all sculptures.

The studios of Gandhara were actively engaged in making Buddhist images from the beginning of the Christian era, and though the Greek rulers of Bactria and Gandhara were deposed by the Kushans, the artistic activity of those areas remained undisturbed. The great Kushan ruler, Kanishka, became an ardent patron of Buddhism, and under his sovereignty the Hellenistic art of Gandhara passed

measure through struggles with cognate peoples, had restored the empire of his famous ancestors and had prepared the way at least for its powerful organization, he attempted, as Herodotus says, ' to explore large parts of Asia.' One of these undertakings was the search for the mouth of the Indus, whither an expedition, under Skylax of Karyanda, was sent. In the later inscriptions of this monarch, the Hindus (Hindu) and the Gandhâras (Gandâra) are mentioned among the subject peoples . . . . . . Under Xerxes, the son and successor of Darius, the Hindu and Gandhâra peoples belonging to the Arkhosian satrapy still owed allegiance to the Persian king ; Indian troops went to Greece with the great army, wintered with Persians and Medes under Mardonios in Thessaly, and sustained with them the defeat of Platæa."

Buddhist art in India, by A. Grünwedel, translated by A. C. Gibson.

all bounds in the production of sculpture. The liberal use of bluish-grey schist (described as horn blend slate), stucco and clay, and the Græco-Roman style, make Gandhara sculptures so distinctive that they can be easily recognised from all other Indian types.

In spite of the dominent Hellenistic influence on style, the Gandhara school in general represented the Indian traditional attitudes, costumes, gestures and the symbolical signs of divinity. The Gandharan Buddha image shows an Apollo-like, soft, fleshy and young head; the *Ushnisha* (the Indian sign of skull protruberence of the sage) is always cleverly concealed by wavy or curly locks of hair; the athletic body of Buddha is suggested even under the heavily folded drapery. Many Buddha and Bodhisattva figures were given a strong moustache, which is never found on any Indian ones. The hosts of Brahminical god, goddesses and demi-gods found at Bharut and Sanchi are present in every Buddhist group. The popularity of the tale of the nativity and renunciation of Buddha is shown by their repeated reproductions. In the relief composition of the former, Mayadevi, the mother of Buddha, stands under a tree holding a branch; she is supported by her sister, Prajapati, and other women in attendance. The child appears from her right flank and the Brahminical god, Indra, in company of other deities, receives the child. The scene of the renunciation depicts the prince seated on a divan by his sleeping wife, Yashodhara, pondering before the great departure. The female musicians and attendants are asleep, crouching over the instruments and the fly-whisks (Fig. 54). The

16

sequel to this is the scene of the exit of the prince on horse-back from the palace, with his faithful servant, Channa, holding fast to the tail of the horse, its hooves borne up by the Yakshas in order to silence the sound. In the *Parinirvana* scene, there is the dramatic setting of the grief-stricken disciples and the Vajrapani (the heavenly attendant of Buddha, carrying a thunder-bolt), lamenting the prone figure of the sage.

These sculptures are mostly in small panels and are carved in schist. The tanagra-type figures of these reliefs, though skilfully arranged and cleverly chiselled, somehow lack spontaneity and life. This may be owing to the mass production of sculptures demanded by the patrons. They are, however, invaluable to history as they reproduced authentic pictures of the people and represent every section of society. Street and interior scenes are shown with typical buildings, conveyances, furniture, utensils and domestic animals. It is the scene of every-day life at that time. Little Greek architecture is shown in Gandhara art except for a few examples of the three orders, especially the Corinthian. The buildings carved in the reliefs are in most cases typically Indian. The large, well-chiselled images of Buddha and Bodhisattva in schist are almost in the round without the supporting portion at the back. The royally garbed figures of the Bodhisattvas appear to have been modelled after the types of the local chieftains (Figs. 57, 58).

It is impossible to classify the periods of progress and decline of this school, since few sculptures bear any helpful inscriptions or a marked difference in style. The common belief is that the sculptures in schist are the earlier examples, and were succeeded by the figures in stucco and clay. The Gandhara school practically ceased at the end of the 5th century A.D., and during its last three centuries produced numerous figures in sun-dried clay with stucco and terra-cotta heads. It was a common practice in Gandhara art to cover stone sculptures with a thin layer of plaster and to enrich them with paint and gilt. Clay figures were decorated similarly. The stucco and terra-cotta heads in several cases may have been casts from moulds. Many of these remarkably modelled heads are excellent specimens of portraiture. They have vigour and a living expression of individuality.

The Gandhara style never crossed the frontier to influence the art of the Indian mainland, though there was some infiltration of motifs and figure composition, as is apparent in Mathura and Amaravati sculptures.* Historically, the most important

* " Neverthless, in spite of its persistency and wide diffusion, Hellenistic art never took the real hold upon India that it took, for example, upon Italy or Western Asia, for the reason that the temperaments of the two peoples were radically dissimilar. To the Greek, man, man's beauty, man's intellect was everything, and it was apotheosis of this beauty and this intellect which still remained the keynote of Hellenistic art even in the Orient. But these ideals awakened no response in the Indian mind. The vision of the Indian was bounded by the immortal rather than the mortal, by the infinite rather than the finite. Where Greek thought was ethical, his was spiritual ; where Greek was rational, his was emotional. And to these higher aspirations, these more spiritual instincts, he sought, at a later date, to give articulate expression by translating them into terms of form and colour."
A guide to Taxila, by Sir John Marshall.

achievement of this school was the introduction of the image of meditating Buddha seated in yogic attitude on a lotus, with half-closed eyes and a perpetual smile. This figure, which became the idol of the entire Buddhist world, appeared simultaneously in Gandhara and Mathura.

VII.

Mathura School (Kushan).

The Kushan king, Kanishka, who ruled from A.D. 120 to A.D. 162, devoted his whole life to the administration of the north-western empire. This was under constant threat from the Parthian, Greek, Scythian and Chinese aggressors. He left the ruling of India proper to his sons, Vasishka and Huvishka, who were allowed the full regal titles. It seems that both of them favoured and encouraged Buddhism as well as Jainism. The great demand for images by the two sects kept the studios of Mathura as active as the Gandhara school.

Mathura, famous as a prosperous and sacred city from the earliest times, became a great centre of Brahminical, Buddhist and Jain faith during the Kushan rule. In this capital city of art, all indigenous and foreign elements were assimilated, and the result was the flowering of classical Indian sculpture at the beginning of the Gupta reign. The sculptors of the Kushan period followed the orthodox tradition of Maurya, Sunga, Bharut and Sanchi art. The chief motives are the familiar Yakshinis under the trees, Bodhisattvas and Nagas, the standing or seated image of Buddha, and the fat and podgy Yaksha king, *Kuvera,* holding the bag of fortune and the wine cup or jug. The presence of a small number of Greek and Roman statuaries has very little significance for this school. Some unusual groups of drunken and bacchanalian statuaries in Mathura art still puzzle the experts. Though carved in orthodox style, they have no clear connection with the religion or myth of the time. It may be that they were introduced by some foreign agent, the identity of which is completely obscured by the Indianised interpretation. Almost every Kushan sculpture in Mathura was executed in mottled red sandstone available in the local quarry. The figures of Kushan Mathura in general lack the refinements of Bharut and Sanchi sculptures. The Kushan Buddha has no locks of hair to adorn his head or the spiral *Ushnisha.* Instead of being seated on the lotus, as in Gandhara work, he rests on a lion-throne which is ornamented by miniature figures of Bodhisattvas and donors at the base. When the figure is shown in a standing attitude, a lion is crouched between the feet. The schematically arranged robes cling to the body, exposing the form. The Buddhas and Bodhisattvas of this school do not show a gentle repose or kindly grace, but express mundane dynamic power.

The Kushan sculptors carried out royal commissions from many ruling monarchs of distant lands, extending to the east and south. Large numbers of figures of this school have been found at Sarnath and Amaravati. The city of Mathura was later ransacked several times by the Islamic invaders, and sculptures were wantonly destroyed. In consequence, only a few examples of its sculptures have survived, and many of them are fragmentary and mutilated. Some of the broken heads belonging to colossal male and female figures show great skill in the portraiture of racial types. The very individualistic head-dress and hair style, and in characteristic expression, show the mastery of Indian genius (Figs. 43, 44, 45). The Yakshinis standing under a tree and a few similar figures with slightly variant poses, exhibit great development on the older motifs (Figs. 38, 39, 40, 41, 42). They boldly stand out from the supporting pillar, revealing sensuous limbs and an exaggerated curvature of the hips. At first sight they appear naked, except for the heavy jewellery. But on closer observation a robe can be seen clinging to the body. These lascivious maidens, some gracefully leaning against a tree, with a raised hand artfully holding a branch, and some in various playful attitudes, are the outstanding examples of the classical school.

VIII.

Amaravati.

While the Gandhara and Mathura schools were flourishing there existed a quite separate school in the south, under the patronage of the Andhra kings, whose rule stretched from sea to sea in south India. The main survival of this period is the remains of the great stupa of Amaravati.

The city of Amaravati was well known in ancient

time and venerated by the Buddhists as a holy place. Evidently in or before the 2nd century B.C. a stupa containing important relics stood at the site where the later one was built. In the course of centuries the later stupa underwent many renovations and additions. The railing and casing slabs, in limestone and containing fine sculptures, were executed during the 2nd century A.D., when the Gandhara motifs reached Amaravati through the intermediary of Kushan art. The illustrations in many reliefs give a good impression of the stupa in its undamaged shape. Except for the fragments of railing, pillar and slabs used for encasing the mound, the remains of this priceless monument are totally lost.

This stupa was similar in shape and setting to those at Bharut and Sanchi, though there was some interesting variation in detail. It is estimated that the railing was 600 feet in circumference and 13 to 14 feet high. The pillars have a full disk in the middle and a half-disk at the top and the bottom, while the rails and the inner faces of the pillars are covered with elaborately carved relief figures. The garland bearing erotes of the coping and the frieze on the plinth, containing animals and dwarfs in comical attitudes, show a clear influence of West-Asian and Gandhara art. Many Kushan sculptures found in Amaravati were either imported from Mathura or executed on the spot by Kushan artists. The figures are beautifully formed and composed, and show a superior knowledge of foreshortening. The procession, court and domestic scenes are full of movement and excitement, and express riotous festivities. The cleverly rendered difficult postures of human and animal figures show the technical mastery of the carvers. The use of both the anthropomorphic image of Buddha and the old symbols representing his presence indicate that they belong to a transition period when the importance of the latter was not minimised by the new idols. The popular motif of 'the woman and the tree,' so prolific in Kushan art, is noticeably rare at Amaravati, but the Nagas still occur frequently in sculptures. Classical Indian figure-art seems to have reached the culmination at Amaravati and, without a marked decline, gradually changes to the medieval style.

XI.

Gupta Art.

The art of the Gupta Empire, established in the 4th century A.D., is the culmination of the art of ancient India.

Palaces and shrines were built entirely in stone masonries, and temples and monasteries were hewn from the rock. There was a revival of the Asokan custom of erecting sculptured monolithic pillars to commemorate great deeds or the holy sites. Few of them, however, have the dignity or excellence of the Maurya ones. At a later period the whole region of the Gupta Empire was occupied by the iconon-clast Islamic armies, who pulled down almost every palace, temple and monastery, and destroyed all works of art that came within their reach. Only a few stone-built temples and rock-cut shrines in remote places survived the disaster. The excavation of Sarnath yielded very valuable finds of Gupta sculpture. This site was an important art centre at the time. The sculptor on the spot used the local beige sandstone, but the presence of many contemporary Mathura sculptures in red stone show that the studios of that city were still maintaining their reputation and skill. The Gupta kings worshipped Brahminical gods and goddesses, but they paid homage to the Buddhist divinities and gave the community unrestricted support.

One of the achievements of the Gupta period was to give each character in mythology, whether Buddhist or Brahminical, certain conventional attitudes and symbolical gestures. A reorganised iconography was established. The mundane, virile and voluptuous images prevalent in the art of Bharut, Sanchi and the Kushan Mathura became gentler and more spiritual. The shaven head of the Kushan Buddha was, under the Guptas, given a short, curly hair. The Gupta artists elaborated his *Mudras* (or the significant hand gestures), conventionalised the extremely diaphanous robe revealing his form, and devised an elaborate decoration for his nimbus and for the lotus or lion throne. Miniature figures of the donors were shown at the base. Another peculiar feature in Gupta sculptures is the curious rendering of webbed fingers found in some Buddha figures. Besides having a mastery of stone carving, the sculptors of this period had a very advanced knowledge of metal casting in *cire perdu* method. The iron pillar in Delhi and the colossal standing Buddha in copper from Sultangung are extraordinary performances of engineering skill and artistic production in metal.

The Gupta art of 6th century A.D. practically concludes the classical tradition, but the convention of the divinity created by the Gupta masters remained the ideals for the later periods in India and influenced the art of all far-eastern countries which came within the orbit of Indian culture.

BIBLIOGRAPHY

COOMARASWAMY, A.   *History of Indian and Indonesian Art*; London, 1927.

CUNNINGHAM, SIR A.   *The Stupa at Bharut*; London, 1879.

FOUCHER, A.   *Beginnings of Buddhist Art*; Paris and London, 1927.

GRUNWEDEL, A.   *Buddhist Art in India*; London, 1901.

MARSHALL, SIR J.   *A Guide to Sanchi*; Calcutta, 1918.
A Guide to Taxila; Delhi, 1936.
The Oxford History of India; Oxford, 1920.

SMITH, V. A.   *Early History of India*; 1924.
A History of Fine Art in India and Ceylon; Oxford, 1930.

TARN, W. W.   *The Greeks in Bactria and India*; Cambridge, 1938.

DESCRIPTIVE NOTES TO THE PLATES

(The illustrations are arranged chronologically with a few exceptions.)

1. BULL CAPITAL of Asoka pillar. Polished sandstone. Height 6ft. 9ins. (205cm.) Provenance: Bihar. *Now at the Indian Museum, Calcutta, India.* 3rd century B.C. Mauryan.

   This remarkable sculpture in the round is an example of the Maurya period. A West-Asian origin is noticeable in the bell-shaped lotus and the frieze of honey-suckle, rosette and palmette reliefs on the abacus. But the animal is of typical Indian breed. It suggests virility combined with gentleness and dignity. Of the excellent carving of this period Sir John Marshall writes: ' The finest carving indeed that India has yet produced, and unsurpassed, I venture to think, by anything of their kind in the ancient world.'

2. YAKSHA. Reddish-grey sandstone. Height 5ft. 5ins. (165cm.) Provenance: Bihar. *Now at Patna Museum, India.* 200 B.C., late Mauryan.

   Although designed to represent a Yaksha, this headless and armless figure portrays a man of humble origin. He carries a fly-whisk. The bulky body, the heavy necklace and armlets, and the schematic loin-cloth tied at the waist with a thick, long belt, constitute an expressing massiveness. Traces of so-called Mauryan polish are still visible on the upper part of the body and on the feet.

3. FEMALE TORSO with ornamental girdle. Terra-cotta. Height 6½ ins. (16cm.) Provenance: Bihar. *Now at Patna Museum, India.* Late 2nd century B.C.

   In this late Maurya or early Sunga statuette, the woman's body is sensitively modelled. This, the drapery, and the elaborate jewellery are full of suggestive colour and warmth of life.

4. MALE FIGURE. Terra-cotta. Height 5½ins. (14cm.) Provenance: Ahichchhatra, U.P. *Now at Central Asian Antiquities Museum, New Delhi, India.* 1st century B.C.

   The elaborate costume and the huge turban of this youthful figure are skilfully shaped and the texture of the fine cloth very well rendered: particularly the part which winds round the right arm and across the body. Though worn out by time, this archaic statuette still retains a fresh and vivid smile.

5. ELEPHANT WITH RIDER. Dark-grey terra-cotta. Height 4¾ins. (14.5cm.) Provenance: Mathura, U.P. *Now at Curzon Museum, Muttra, India.* 2nd century B.C.

6. HEAD OF A MAN. Sandstone. Height 6ins. (15cm.) Provenance: Sarnath, U.P. *Now at Sarnath Museum, India.* Early 2nd century B.C. Sunga

27

This portrait head with a long, curly moustache may be of a donor. Though it lacks the precision in chiselling of the Asokan masters, it expresses vigour and massive monumental quality.

7 – 8. YAKSHI. Polished sandstone. Height (without base) 5ft. 3ins. (160cm.) Provenance: Bihar. *Now at Patna Museum, India.* 1st century B.C.

It is curious that the upper half of this figure shows refined modelling of an advanced sculpture and the lower half maintains the archaic frontality, see page 7.

9. RAILING OF BHARUT (fragment). Red standstone. Height 9ft. (274cm.) Provenance: Bharut. *Now at Indian Museum, Calcutta, India.* 2nd century B.C.

The railing of Bharut when complete had numerous pillars, rectangular in section, joined together by lenticular cross-bars. These bars were arranged vertically, three in each section mortised into the pillars on either side, and over the pillars were laid huge coping stones. The left end pillar of the illustration shows a royal personage on an elephant. He is holding a relic. On his left is a horseman who is carrying an elaborate banner with an interesting figure of a man-bird (Garuda). The upper disk on the rail contains the image of Laksmi or Sri—the goddess of fortune.

10. A BAS RELIEF on Bharut pillar. Red sandstone. Width 1ft. 8ins. (51cm.) Provenance: Bharut. *Now at Indian Museum, Calcutta, India.* 2nd century B.C.

This depicts the dream of Mayadevi. The divine Bodhisattva Sakyamuni (i.e., the spirit of Buddha) descends from heaven in the shape of a white elephant and approaches the queen, who is asleep on a couch with attendants arround. A lamp is shown burning, to indicate that it is a night scene.

11. BAS RELIEF on the coping. Red sandstone. Provenance: Bharut. *Now at Indian Museum, Calcutta, India.* 2nd century B.C.

This represents the story of four exiled princes. The sage Kapila grants their request to give up his hermitage to be the site of their new city which was named Kapilavasthu. The sage is seen here with matted hair coiled behind his head after the usual manner of ascetics. The four princes stand and kneel with their hands joined in respectful attitudes.

12. GANGITA YAKSHA. Red sandstone. Height 5ft. (152cm.) Provenance: Bharut. *Now at Indian Museum, Calcutta, India.* 2nd century B.C.

This archaic figure represents a demi-god. His high position is shown by the elephant and the tree under his feet.

13. CHULAKOKA DEVATA. Red sandstone. Height 5ft. (152cm.) Provenance: Bharut. *Now at Indian Museum, Calcutta, India.* 2nd century B.C.

See page 13.

14. SIRIMA DEVATA. Red sandstone. Height 5ft. (152cm.) Provenance: Bharut. *Now at Indian Museum, Calcutta, India.* 2nd century B.C.

This remarkably plastic and archaic figure probably represents the ancient mother-goddess. Compared with similar figures, this piece of sculpture is very well formed and neatly chiselled. Notice the carving of the diaphanous costume and jewellery. The very naturalistic right hand probably held a lotus.

15. THE JETAVANA MONASTERY. Red sandstone. Width 1ft. 8ins. (51cm.) Provenance: Bharut. *Now at Indian Museum, Calcutta, India.* 2nd century B.C.

16. DETAIL FROM A PILLAR. Red sandstone. Provenance: Bharut. *Now at Indian Museum, Calcutta, India.* 2nd century B.C.

This depicts the Apsaras who are performing a dance and playing music in heaven. Harps, cymbals and one or two other musical instruments whose nature is difficult to explain can be seen illustrated in this relief.

17. WEST GATE. Sandstone. Provenance: Sanchi. 1st century B.C. Shows part of the hemispherical dome and the encircling railing and the gate.

18. DETAILS OF A PILLAR (East gate). Sandstone. Provenance: Sanchi. 1st century B.C.

The bas reliefs illustrate the Jatak stories.

19. DETAILS OF A PILLAR (North gate). Sandstone. Provenance: Sanchi. 1st century B.C.

20. DETAILS OF A PILLAR (East gate). Sandstone. Provenance: Sanchi. 1st century B.C.

21. DETAILS OF A PILLAR (North gate). Sandstone. Provenance: Sanchi. 1st century B.C.

22. ARCHITRAVES (North gate). Sandstone. Provenance: Sanchi. 1st century B.C.

The four elephants on the top carried a wheel of the law, a fragment of which still exists on the left.

23. MIDDLE ARCHITRAVE (West Gate). Sandstone. Provenance: Sanchi. 1st century B.C.

Depicts the first preaching Buddha in the deer-park. In the centre is the ' Wheel of the Law ' and on both sides are devotees in reverential attitudes.

24. THE CHADDANTA JATAKA (West gate, front view, lower architrave). Sandstone. Provenance: Sanchi. 1st century B.C.

This relates a story of Bodhisattva (Bodhisattva is the name for Buddha in his incarnations previous to his last birth), when he was born as a king of the elephants. One of his two wives bore a grudge against him, and after her death she was reborn and became the queen of Benares. Remembering the past, she feigned an illness and told the king that only the tusks of the elephant-king will cure her. Eventually the elephant was hunted and killed, and the tusks were secured and brought before the queen. But on seeing the tusks she was overtaken with remorse and she died broken-hearted.

The bulky and uncouth animals are here beautifully grouped in the panel. Elephant king is shown with six tusks and with the attendant elephants holding the royal umbrella and the fly-whisk to mark his royalty.

25. MIDDLE ARCHITRAVE (West gate). Sandstone. Provenance: Sanchi. 1st century B.C.

Depicts Buddha departing from Kapilavastu, the city of his birth. His presence is represented by the umbrella held over the empty saddle on the horse and by the footprint. The progress of the horse is shown by its figure being several times repeated.

26. DETAILS OF LOWER ARCHITRAVE (North gate). Sandstone. Provenance: Sanchi. 1st century B.C.

Shows a part of a palace with the city wall and the watchtowers. The trees and lotuses in the foreground suggest the moat, and on the right, two women are seen emerging from the city gate.

27. DETAIL (North gate). Sandstone. Provenance: Sanchi. 1st century B.C.

28. DETAIL (East gate). Sandstone. Provenance: Sanchi. 1st century B.C.

A forest scene depicting water-buffaloes, deer and birds.

29. FLOWER MOTIFS (North gate). Sandstone. Provenance: Sanchi. 1st century B.C.

Lotuses and the vessel with holy water.

30. FLOWER MOTIFS (North gate). Sandstone. Provenance: Sanchi. 1st century B.C.

Lotuses and the vessel with holy water.

31. TWO PEACOCKS (North gate). Sandstone. Provenance: Sanchi. 1st century B.C.

32. WINGED DEER (North gate). Sandstone. Provenance: Sanchi. 1st century B.C.

These winged animals perhaps are of Persepolitan origin.

33. YAKSHINI (North gate). Sandstone. Provenance: Sanchi. 1st century B.C.

Caryatid type figure carved in the round. She is seen playfully holding on to the trunk and the branches of a tree, and is almost nude except for the transparent garment round the lower limbs. The figure suggests a ' memory picture ' closely resembling the types found in Bharut art.

34. **LAKSHMI or SRI** (East gate). Sandstone. Provenance: Sanchi. 1st century B.C.
    See page 5.

35. **CAMELS WITH RIDERS** (East gate). Sandstone. Provenance: Sanchi. 1st century B.C.

36. **BULLS WITH RIDERS** (East gate). Sandstone. Provenance: Sanchi. 1st century B.C.

37. **JAINA AYAGAPATA.** Red sandstone. Height 2ft. 1in. (63cm.). Provenance: Mathura, U.P. *Now in Provincial Museum, Lucknow, India.* 1st century A.D.
    'An Ayagapata is an ornamental slab, bearing the representation of a Jina or some other object of worship, and the term may be appropriately rendered by "tablet of homage or worship" since such slabs were put up in temples, as the numerous inscriptions say, "for the worship of the Arhats." *Epigraphia Indica,* Vol. 11.

38. **WOMAN AND CHILD.** Red sandstone. Height 2ft. 1in. (63cm.) Provenance: Mathura, U.P. *Now at Curzon Museum, Muttra, India.* Late 1st century A.D.
    The woman appears to be holding a rattle or similar object and the child is trying to catch it. The simple and clear pattern of the composition is well harmonised. The elaborate coiffeurs, drapery and jewellery do not suffer from over intricate details. The attitude is easy and naturalistic. The girl whose head appears above the curtain at the back seems to be watching the game of the mother and child.

39. **FEMALE FIGURE.** Red sandstone. Height 3ft. 10ins. (116cm.) Provenance: Mathura, U.P. *Now at Prov. Museum, Lucknow, India.* Early 2nd century A.D.
    Probably belongs to the ancient cult of mother-goddess. The attitude of touching the breast with the left hand may symbolise fertility. An advance from the frontal and archaic sculptures of Bharut and Sanchi is clearly seen in the naturalistic poise and movement. Though the 'memory picture' was still in vogue, the figure has the look of a realistic sensuous living human body.

40. **FEMALE PALACE GUARD.** Red sandstone. Height 2ft. 10ins. (86cm.) Provenance: Mathura, U.P. *Now at Prov. Museum, Lucknow, India.* 2nd century A.D.
    This figure is very much the same in pattern as the 'woman and the tree' motifs of Bharut and Sanchi sculptures, except that she is holding a broad sword on the left hand. Compared with the elegant modelling of the top part of the body, the legs are rather crudely shaped and weak.

41. **WOMAN WITH CLASPED HANDS.** Red sandstone. Provenance: Mathura, U.P *Now at Prov. Museum, Lucknow, India.* 2nd century A.D.

31

42. GIRL CARRYING BIRD-CAGE. Red sandstone. Height 4ft. 3ins. (129cm.) Provenance: Mathura, U.P. *Now at Indian Museum, Calcutta, India.* Early 2nd century A.D.

The figure is nude except that there is a suggestion of transparent cloth. A bird is perched on the girl's left arm and is seen pecking her hair. The girl holds the cage in her right hand. It is difficult to explain the significance of the dwarfish monster crouched under her feet. On the balcony above the girl's head, two women can be seen engaged in their toilet.

43. MAN'S HEAD. Red sandstone. Height 11ins. (27cm.) Provenance: Mathura, U.P. *Now at Curzon Museum, Muttra, India.* 2nd century A.D.

This is a portrait head and is part of a colossal figure. The rich turban, the individualistic features, and the dignified bearing of the face suggest that the man is a royal personage or a nobleman.

44. GIRL'S HEAD. Red sandstone. Height 1ft. 2½ins. (36.5cm.) Provenance: Mathura, U.P. *Now at Curzon Museum, Muttra, India.* 2nd century A.D.

This portrait head of a colossal figure perhaps represents a Yakshi or a lady of noble origin. Though badly damaged, the sensitive form and fine and delicate rendering of the coiffure are still visible.

45. GIRL'S HEAD. Red sandstone. Height 4¾ins. (12cm.) Provenance: Mathura, U.P. *Now at British Museum, London.* Early 2nd century A.D.

46. MAN AND WOMEN. Red sandstone. Height 1ft. 2¼ins. (36cm.) Provenance: Sarguja, C.P. *Now at Indian Museum, Calcutta, India.* Late 2nd century A.D.

This group is somewhat crudely carved in comparison with the figures on the railing pillars. The little woman on the left is not meant to be a dwarf. She is of less importance or humbler rank than the other two figures. It is hard to explain the story this group represents.

47. BODHISATTVA. Red sandstone. Height 5ft. 10ins. (177cm.) Provenance: unknown. *Now at Curzon Museum, Muttra, India.* Early 2nd century A.D.

This huge and headless figure continues the static monumental style of the figures found at Bharut and Sanchi, but its modelling is more refined and well constructed. It suggests great power. The extremely diaphanous robe, gathering below the knee in formal pattern and with part falling between the legs, adds to the stability and monolithic height of the figure.

48. FRAGMENT OF ARCH. Red sandstone. Height 3ft. 1in. (94cm.) Provenance: Mathura, U.P. *Now at Curzon Museum, Muttra, India.* 2nd century A.D.
   The bas reliefs on this stone arch show the adoration of Buddha and Bodhisattva.

49. NUDE GODDESS. Terra-cotta. Height 4¾ins. (12.3cm.) Provenance: Taxila. *Now in the collection of Col. D. H. Gordon, D.S.O., O.B.E., Hingham, Norfolk.* Early 1st century A.D.

50. WINGED FEMALE FIGURE (brooch). Gold epousé. Height 3¼ins. (8.3cm.) Provenance: Sirkap, W. Punjab. *Now at Central Asian Antiquities Museum, New Delhi, India.* 1st-2nd century A.D.

51. FEMALE FIGURE. Serpentine. Provenance: Taxila. *Now at Central Asian Antiquities Museum, New Delhi, India.* Early 2nd century A.D.
   This figure holding a lotus shows Graeco-Roman workmanship applied to an Indian pattern. The attitude, the transparent robe revealing the curve of the body, and the heavy girdle could easily be compared with the prototypes of this figure from Bharut and Muthura. But the face, coiffure and the naturalistic body have a Hellenistic form.

52. MALE HEAD. Terra-cotta. Height 8½ins. (21.5cm.) Provenance: Gandhara. *Now in the Indian Section, Victoria and Albert Museum, London.* 2nd century A.D.
   This Hellenistic head shows naturalistic hair style and features. Such individualistic expression is seldom found in purely Indian productions.

53. RENUNCIATION. Schist. Height 11¾ins. (31cm.) Provenance: Gandhara. *Now at Peshawar Museum, Pakistan.* 2nd-4th century A.D.
   This scene shows Prince Shiddhartha (Buddha) about to leave the side of his sleeping wife and mount his horse. His faithful attendant, Channa or Chandaka, is seen holding the rein of the horse. The figures are grouped harmoniously but the carving lacks the technical refinement of the later art of Gandhara.

54. RENUNCIATION. Schist. Height 2ft. 0½ins. (62cm.) Provenance: Gandhara. *Now at Central Museum, Lahore, Pakistan.* 2nd-4th century A.D.
   The prince is seen, seated on the divan, by his sleeping wife. He is pondering before the ' great departure.' The musicians are seen asleep in the foreground. The gods and Bodhisattvas are witnessing the great event from above. The bull represents Taurus constellations indicating the time at which Buddha rode away from home. The architecture shown in this relief is of Indian type but the figures and the draperies are Hellenistic.

55. **FRIEZE OF WORSHIPPERS.** Serpentine. Height 6¼ins. (16cm.) Provenance: unknown. *Now at Peshwar Museum, Pakistan.* 2nd-4th century A.D.

56. **THE PARINIRVANA.** Schist. Height 1ft. 4ins. (41cm.) Provenance: unknown. *Now in the Indian Section, Victoria and Albert Museum, London.* 2nd-3rd century A.D.

This is the lower portion of a complete scene. It had the recumbent figure of Buddha lying on a draped couch covering the whole length of this frieze. It shows Vajrapani (the thunderbolt carrier on the left) and other disciples of Buddha lamenting his passing away. The figure on the right seated in meditation may be Subhadra, the last converted disciple of Buddha, and the object hanging from a tripod may be his alms-bowl.

57. **MAITREYA.** Schist. Height 3ft. 5½ins. (105cm.) Provenance: Gandhara. *Now in the collection of Messrs. Spink & Sons Ltd., London.* 2nd-4th century.

He is one of the Bodhisattvas, the future Messiah, who, like Buddha, is destined to preach the Law and bring peace. His left leg is slightly bent forward. The raised right hand (now missing) held a part of the scarf, and the left hand holds the vessel with sacred water. The large loop of knotted hair on his head is peculiar to all Gandhara Maitreya. He bears on his forehead the ' Urna,' a divine symbol which is found in all Gandhara Buddhas and Bodhisattvas. He has a strong moustache. The heavy necklace has a clasp of female centaurs.

58. **BODHISATTVA.** Schist. Height 4ft. 3⅛ins. (130cm.) Provenance: Gandhara. *Now at Peshawar Museum, Pakistan.* 2nd-4th century A.D.

He wears a rich turban. The lost right hand probably showed 'Abhaya Mudra' (gesture of protection). Besides necklace, he is wearing a string of amulets across his body. His right foot is slightly bent forward and he wears strapped sandals on his feet. The pedestal contains a pair of Corinthian pillars on the sides. Figures of devotees and the wheel or the lotus symbol are shown in the middle.

59. **CHARIOT OF THE LESSER VEHICLE** (Hinayana). Schist. Height 1ft. 0½in. (32cm.) Provenance: Gandhara. *Now in the Indian Section, Victoria and Albert Museum, London.* 4th-5th century A.D.

This generally accepted title may be wrong. Perhaps it really depicts the Bodhisattva with other children going to school. The wooden tablets which the figures are carrying are still used for writing in village schools in India. Besides the tablets, they are also carrying the ink-pots.

60. **SEATED BUDDHA.** Schist. Height 3ft. 7½ins. (110cm.) Provenance: Gandhara. *Now at The Royal Scottish Museum, Edinburgh, Scotland.* 3rd-4th century A.D..

34

Under the folds of the robe is shown the robust body of an athlete. He is seated on a lion-throne, which contains figures of Bodhisattvas and disciples in miniature. The extreme right figure on the throne is that of a Buddhist nun. The neat chiselling, balanced proportion and well-shaped form of the figure show the fine sculptural achievement of the Gandharan art.

61. SEATED BUDDHA. Stucco. Height 2ft. (61cm.) Provenance: Gandhara. *Now in the collection of Captain Hay of Hayfield, Lerwick, Shetland.* 2nd-4th century A.D.

In comparison with the Fig. No. 7, this looks decadent and the robe and the form are crudely shaped.

62. HEAD OF YOUTH. Stucco. Height 11ins. (28cm.) Provenance: Gandhara. *Now in the Indian Section, Victoria and Albert Museum, London.* 4th-5th century A.D.

This superbly modelled head with masses of curly hair is an excellent example of vivacious youth.

63. HEAD OF BODHISATTVA. Stucco. Provenance: Gandhara. *Now in the Indian Section, Victoria and Albert Museum, London.* 4th-5th century A.D.

64. MALE HEAD. Stucco. Height 6½ins. (17cm.) Provenance: Gandhara. *Now in the collection of Captain Hay of Hayfield, Lerwick, Shetland.* 5th century A.D.

65. MALE HEAD. Stucco. Height 5¼ins. (13.5cm.) Provenance: Gandhara. *Now in the Indian Section, Victoria and Albert Museum, London.* 4th-5th century A.D.

This shaven-hair very Graeco-Roman head may be that of a Buddhist monk.

66. HEAD OF AN ASCETIC. Terra-cotta. Height 3¼ins. (9cm.) Provenance: Gandhara. *Now in the collection of Col. D. H. Gordon, D.S.O., O.B.E.* 5th century A.D.

67. HEAD OF A YOUNG MAN. Terra-cotta. Height 5½ins. (14cm.) Provenance: Jammu, Kashmir. *Now at Central Museum, Lahore, Pakistan.* 6th-7th century A.D.

68. FRAGMENT OF FRIEZE. Limestone. Height 2ft. 3ins. (68.5cm.) Provenance: Amaravati. *Now at British Museum, London.* 2nd century A.D.

The left side of this frieze shows the worship of a relic mound. On the right is the interior scene of a nobleman's house. A halo is shown behind the head of the woman. She may represent Mayadevi. There is a fine pictorial quality in this relief. A similar composition of figures and similar interior details are found in the wall paintings at the rock temples of Ajanta.

69. SCULPTURED PILLAR (details). Limestone. Provenance: Amaravati. *Now at British Museum, London.* 2nd century A.D.

The centre of this pillar shows the five hooded Naga. On either side of him are two females bearing offerings and standing on two reptilian monsters.

70. **BAS RELIEF.** Limestone. Height 4ft. 1½ins. (126 cm.) Provenance: Amaravati. *Now at British Museum, London.* 2nd century A.D.

The story of this relief is not clear. The upper scene depicts a man with two wives, two friends, a horse and an elephant. He is probably meant to be contrasted with the king at the lower relief who, with the full rank of great king, is possessed of seven precious things—the treasures of the Wheel, elephant, a horse, a wife, pearls, attendant and a councillor. The modelling of the figures show the superior skill of the Amaravati masters.

71. **NATIVITY OF BUDDHA.** Limestone. Height 2ft. (61cm.) Provenance: Amaravati. *Now at British Museum, London.* 2nd century A.D.

This relief depicts Mayadevi standing on the right, holding on to a branch of the tree. The gods on her right are in the attitude of receiving the child. On the left of the panel is a woman carrying the child, whose presence is represented by the symbol of a footprint. A Yaksha king emerging from a tree is paying homage to the infant Buddha.

72. **BAS RELIEF.** Limestone. Height 1ft. 10½ins. (57cm.) Provenance: Amaravati. *Now at Government Museum, Madras, India.* 2nd century A.D.

This relief on the rail bar depicts the playful frolic of a 'Gana' or a dwarf with a bull and a mythical winged animal. The motif is of West-Asian origin but the bull is a perfect representation of an Indian breed.

73. **FRIEZE.** Limestone. Height 2ft. (61cm.) Provenance: Amaravati. *Now at British Museum, London.* 2nd century A.D.

The reliefs show probably Jataka scenes but their stories are not clear. The robes on the figures show the influence of the Gandhara style.

74. **RENUNCIATION.** Limestone. Height 1ft. 4ins. (41cm.) Provenance: Amaravati. *Now at British Museum, London.* 2nd century A.D.

The scene on the right depicts Prince Shiddhartha, who is seated on a couch, and around him are the female attendants asleep in ungainly attitudes. The scene on the left is the 'great departure' of the prince. The gods and the divine spirits are seen rejoicing the event. Prince Shiddhartha's faithful attendant, Channa or Chandaka, is seen leading the horse, holding it by its bridle. The dwarfish Yakshas are shown bearing the hooves of the horse to silence the noise.

This frieze shows excellent modelling and superb composition.

75. **STUPA.** Limestone. Height 3ft. 9ins. (114.5cm.) Provenance: Amaravati. *Now at British Museum, London.* 2nd century A.D.

This illustration of a stupa shows the five hooded Naga in the centre. The railing and pillars are covered with lotuses. On the top of the stupa there is a decorative cluster of umbrellas.

76. DECORATIVE BAS RELIEF. Limestone. Height 1ft. 9ins. (52.5cm.) Provenance: Amaravati. *Now at British Museum, London.* 2nd-4th century A.D.

77. SCULPTURED DISK. Limestone. Width 2ft. 8½ins. (82cm.) Provenance: Amaravati. *Now at British Museum, London.* 2nd century A.D.

This shows a relic-casket placed on a throne under a rich canopy. It is being worshipped by the Naga king and his people. The excellent perspective of the throne shows how well-developed the stupa art was, compared with that of Bharut and Sanchi.

78. SCULPTURED DISK. Limestone. Width 2ft. 8½ins. (82cm.) Provenance: Amaravati. *Now at British Museum, London.* 2nd century A.D.

Depicts a musical entertainment. Two noblemen are seated on a sofa listening to a concert performed by a number of women in the foreground. Three women are playing on harps, three or four on drums, three on flutes and on various instruments whose nature it is difficult to make out.

79. SCULPTURED PILLAR. Limestone. Height 4ft. (122cm.) Provenance: Amaravati. *Now at British Museum, London.* 2nd century A.D.

In the top circle, prince Shiddhartha is seen riding away from the city gate. He is shown with his full rank of king, with the State umbrella borne over his head, the fly-whisk bearers at his side, and musicians and dancers preceding the procession. The distinguishing mark of a saint—a halo round the head—is found in this stupa sculpture for the first time. No halo is depicted either in Bharut or Sanchi. In the lower relief, the central scene depicts prince Shiddhartha in court and a man kissing his feet. Others are shown in reverential attitudes. On the left is a man bearing a relic on a tray. On the right is shown the worship of the Wheel. There are two antelopes in the foreground, and these represent the first preaching of Buddha in the deer-park.

80. SCULPTURED PILLAR. Limestone. Height 5ft. 9ins. (176cm.) Provenance: Amaravati. *Now at British Museum, London.* 2nd century A.D.

On the top is a king seated on his throne with councillors in attendance. He seems to be reviewing an army parade which is sallying from the city gate. In front of the army, the infantry is advancing. In the foreground, an enemy seems to have fallen on his knees to beg mercy.

81. MALE HEAD. Terra-cotta. Height 1½ins. (3.3cm.) Provenance: Hyderabad State. *Now at Government Museum, Hyderabad, India.* 2nd-3rd century A.D.

This powerful statuette, though small, has all the qualities of monumental sculpture. The simplified structure of the body and the heroically raised head combine realism and vigour. The heavy ear-rings seemed to be in the form of a reptilian figure.

82. SEATED BUDDHA. Sandstone. Height 2ft. 4½ins. (72cm.)
Provenance: Sarnath. *Now at Sarnath Museum, India.* 5th
century A.D.

Headless image of Buddha showing the symbolical hand gesture
expressing the 'Wheel of the Law' or the first preaching. The
robe clings to the body as in the Maurya and Bharut and Sanchi
styles. The frieze on the throne contains 'The Wheel' on a
lotus, with two deer representing the first preaching at the deer-
park. There are five disciples seated in reverential attitudes.

83. TORSO OF BODHISATTVA. Red sandstone. Height 2ft.
10½ins. (87cm.) Provenance: Sanchi. *Now in the Indian Section,
Victoria and Albert Museum, London.* 5th century A.D.

This torso shows the culmination of classical sculpture. The
elaborately carved necklace, shoulder strap and drapery, and the
band round the waist show highly skilled craftsmanship. There
is no suggestion of athletic muscles as in the Gandharan art, and
though the form has been idealised, it has all the beauties of a
vigorous but controlled strength.

84. BUDDHA. Red sandstone. Height 7ft. 1½ins. (217cm.) Provenance: Mathura, U.P. *Now at Indian Museum, Calcutta, India.*
5th century A.D.

This figure of the standing Buddha has the slim but well-
covered body of an ascetic. The small head of the figure accen-
tuates the height. It has a gentle and sublime expression. The
diaphanous cloak reveals the form under the schematic folds.
The nimbus is very richly decorated.

85. BUDDHA. Bronze. Height 7ft. 4½ins. (225cm.) Provenance:
Sultangung, Bhagalpur Dist. *Now at Birmingham Museum and
Art Gallery, Birmingham.* 5th century A.D.

This almost intact colossal image of Buddha, cast in Cire
perdue, shows the engineering skill of the Gupta masters and
their artistry in metal. The figure wears the transparent cloak of
an ascetic, as in the stone image, No. 84. There is no pronounced
suggestion of muscles, and the limbs are simplified and subor-
dinated to iconographic purposes. The right hand shows the
'Abhaya Mudra' (gesture of protection).

86. FLYING GANDHARVAS. Sandstone. Height 2ft. 8½ins. (82cm.)
Provenance: Gwalior. *Now at Archæological Museum, Gwalior,
India.* 6th century A.D.

This represents the heavenly musicians and dancers, the 'Gandharvas' flying in the air. The motion of flying is shown by the
drawn legs and the wind-swept draperies. The head-dress of the
figures is highly decorative. After 6th century A.D., the sculpture
in India became very decorative and the increased ornamentation
of the head-dress, robe and jewellery overburdened and weakened
the structure of human form.

1. Bull capital, Asoka pillar, BIHAR

2. Yaksha, male torso, BIHAR

3. Female torso, BIHAR

5. Elephant with rider, MATHURA

4. Male figure, AHICHCHHATRA

6. Head of a man, SARNATH

7. Yakshi, BIHAR

8. Yakshi, BIHAR

9. Railing, BHARUT

10. Bas relief on pillar, BHARUT

11. Bas relief on coping, BHARUT

12. Gangita Yaksha, BHARUT   13. Chulakoka Devata, BHARUT

14. Sirima Devata, BHARUT

16. Details from a pillar, BHARUT

15. The Jetavana Monastery, BHARUT

17. West gate, SANCHI

18. Pillar, East gate, SANCHI   19. Pillar, North gate, SANCHI

20. Pillar, East gate, SANCHI   21. Pillar, North gate, SANCHI

22. Architraves of North gate, SANCHI

23. Middle architrave of West gate, SANCHI

24. The Chaddanta Jataka, lower architrave, SANCHI

25. Middle architrave of West gate, SANCHI

28. Detail of East gate, SANCHI

27. North gate, SANCHI

26. Detail of lower architrave, North gate, SANCHI

29. Flower motifs, North gate, SANCHI

30. Flower motifs, North gate, SANCHI

31. Two peacocks, North gate, SANCHI

32. Winged deer, North gate, SANCHI

33. Yakshini, North gate, SANCHI

34. Lakshmi or Sri, East gate, SANCHI

35. Camels with riders, East gate, SANCHI

36. Bulls with riders, East gate, SANCHI

37.   Jaina Ayagapata, MATHURA

38. Woman and child, MATHURA

39. Female figure, MATHURA

Female palace guard, MATHURA

41. Woman with clasped hands, MATHURA

42. Girl carrying bird cage, MATHURA

43. Man's head, MATHURA

44. Girl's head, MATHURA

45. Girl's head, MATHURA

46. Man and women, SARGUJA

47. Bodhisattva, provenance unknown

48. Fragment of arch, MATHURA

49. Nude goddess, TAXILA

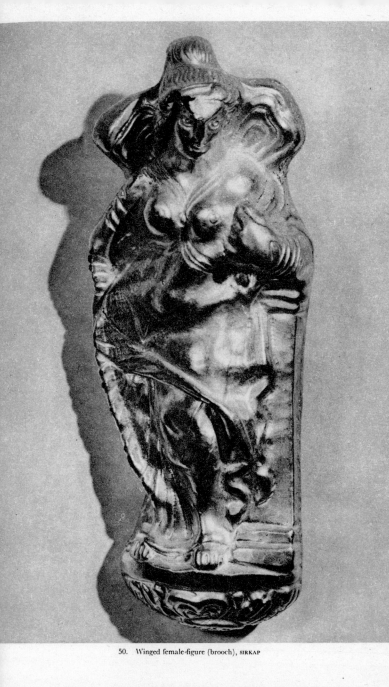

50. Winged female-figure (brooch), SIRKAP

51. Female figure, TAXILA

52.   Male head, GANDHARA

53. Renunciation, GANDHARA

54. Renunciation, GANDHARA

55. Frieze of worshippers, provenance unknown

56. The Parinirvana, provenance unknown

57. Maitreya, GANDHARA

58. Bodhisattva, GANDHARA

59. Chariot of the Lesser Vehicle, GANDHARA

60. Seated Buddha, GANDHARA

61. Seated Buddha, GANDHARA

62. Head of youth, GANDHARA

63.   Head of Bodhisattva, GANDHARA

64.   Male head, GANDHARA

65. Male head, GANDHARA

66. Head of an ascetic, GANDHARA

67. Head of a young man, JAMMU

68. Fragment of frieze, AMARAVATI

69.   Sculptured pillar, detail, AMARAVATI

70. · Bas relief, AMARAVATI

71. Nativity of Buddha, AMARAVATI

72. Bas relief, AMARAVATI

73. Frieze, AMARAVATI

74. Renunciation, AMARAVATI

76. Decorative bas relief, AMARAVATI

75. Stupa, AMARAVATI

77, 78. Sculptured disks, AMARAVATI

79. Sculptured pillar, AMARAVATI

80. Sculptured pillar, AMARAVATI

81. Male head, HYDERABAD STATE

82. Seated Buddha, SARNATH

83. Torso of Bodhisattva, SANCHI

84. Buddha, MATHURA

85. Buddha, SULTANGUNG

86. Flying Gandharvas, GWALIOR